IMPORTANT THINGS IN LIFE

ALISON RHODES

AUGUR PRESS

IMPORTANT THINGS IN LIFE

Copyright © Alison Rhodes 2016

The moral right of the author has been asserted

British Library Cataloguing in Publication Data.
A catalogue record for this book is available from
the British Library.

ISBN 978-1-911229-01-8

First published 2016 by
Augur Press
Delf House
52 Penicuik Road
Roslin
Midlothian EH25 9LH
United Kingdom

Printed by Lightning Source

Dedication

To Gary and Joshua
Thank you for your constant love, help and support.

To my Mum and Dad
Who are always there for us all.

I am so grateful that you are all in my life.

To all facing illness and hard times, in particular
Scleroderma Warriors.

And to all angel babies born too soon.

ANGEL CHILD

A part of my life
You were meant to be
But will now only live
Forever in my memory.

Never did I hear
You laugh or cry.
No chance to hold you
Before I had to say goodbye.

You changed my life forever
Though most will never know.
Your life started growing within me
But too soon you had to go.

You are still so precious;
My love's so tender and mild.
I promise to never forget you,
My darling Angel Child.

Love, Mummy xxx

Contents

SIGHT

The things we take for granted,
The things we see each day.
The things we've always wanted –
Let's close our eyes and pray.

Pray that they'll remain here
Until our lives have passed.
The little things that seem mere
And yet they are so vast.

The colour of leaves in Autumn,
All red and brown and gold.
Such things that are so small to some,
To others are so bold.

And so let's count our blessings
That they're here for us to see.
They may not seem significant
But they mean the world to me.

Alison Walton (now Rhodes)
1985, aged 14-15 years

Introduction

I've always found writing my thoughts down very therapeutic and from a young age I discovered that I would often automatically write in rhyme.

I didn't find the courage to share my writing with anyone until, at High School when I was 15, our English Teacher asked us to write a poem about 'Sight'. It was very poignant as my Mum had recently been diagnosed with a disease that would gradually rob her of her sight, so I wrote from my heart. When our teacher said she had "a particularly beautiful poem that had been handed in and wanted to read it to the class", I was amazed when it was mine!

As life became busier with work, marriage, and so on, I found that it was at the saddest times of my life that I would feel compelled to put pen to paper. When I devastatingly miscarried our first much-wanted, long-awaited baby, I took some comfort from writing poems for her and then when our incredibly precious son arrived I was able to see the world through the eyes of a child again and wanted to convey the magic around us in my writing.

In 2010 I trained to be a Reiki Healing Practitioner and, in order to get to know the others in the class better, we were asked to tell a little about ourself and our interests. I mentioned that I wrote poetry and though I was reluctant at first, I was persuaded to share some with the group. The teachings I received from the course gave me more confidence and self-belief, things I had been distinctly lacking, and helped me to regain a sense of inner peace which was then reflected in the type of things I wrote about.

I wrote the poems in this collection over a period of more than four years – from 25 January 2012 (*Before your life is through*) to 22 June 2016 (*Survive and thrive together*).

In March 2013, I went to bed one night feeling absolutely fine and awoke the next morning barely able to move, with no feeling at all in my right arm. I spent a few months in absolute agony, unable to use my hands, I wasn't able to do much for myself and could hardly walk before I was eventually diagnosed with Rheumatoid Arthritis. Treatment began easing things a little but the following year I was dealt a second blow when I was told that I also have Scleroderma, a rare disease for which there is currently no cure. I decided then that I couldn't give up. I had to fight all the way. I wanted to help raise awareness and use my experiences to help others who are encountering hardships to understand that our mind is a powerful tool and whatever life brings, we can choose not to dwell on the negatives and find something positive to focus on. The illnesses reduced my physical capacity profoundly. They can often be life-limiting and drastically reduce life expectancy. I have chosen to let them give me a new perspective on life – how we have to cherish everybody and every moment while we still can.

If, through my words, I can encourage even just one other person to connect more deeply with life's riches, and develop new optimism, my life won't have been in vain. I have selected the poems for this collection specifically because I have a passionate wish to help others to benefit from the very precious help and guidance I have received.

Alison L Rhodes

A MORNING BLESSING

Shades of pink and orange
Streak across the sky;
I hear the whistle of a dove's wings
As it passes by.

So many blessings,
As another day unfolds.
There is beauty everywhere
For the eye to behold.

Listening to the gentle whisper
Spoken from the trees,
As they sway gently,
In the morning breeze.

A whole new day is dawning,
Full of hope and love.
Make the most of every moment,
It's a gift from up above.

CREATING OUR FUTURE

If we could catch a glimpse of our future
Would we really want to know
What is on its way for us,
What life has in store?

Could we, in any way, influence
The path that we would take?
Would we choose to change the course
Of the journey we would make?

If we saw things we hadn't anticipated
Would we try to resist?
Only to find that the original path
Would, simply, still persist?

As everything happens for a reason,
We are exactly where we should be
At any particular moment;
That's all we need to see.

Even when the road seems difficult
It will lead us to where we need to go.
Acceptance is the key of life,
So relax and go with the flow.

If we trust in our own heart's guidance
We will not go wrong.
Always listen to your inner voice,
Your self-belief should be strong.

If you feel that you're not worthy
Of the blessings coming to you,
Then, you stand in your own way
Of making your dreams come true.

YOU ARE ENOUGH

Sometimes life appears hard
And the road ahead seems rough.
We feel that we've lost our way
And believe we're not enough.

There are times, in this big, wide world
When we start to feel so small;
Unimportant, insignificant,
We stumble and we fall.

We fill our minds with doubts
By worrying too much.
We enrobe ourselves in darkness
And, from reality, we lose touch.

We feel our world is shattering
And allow the tears to fall.
Believing we've let ourselves down,
We give up on it all.

But we have to learn to accept
That it can be all right not to be okay.
Our emotions should be used as lessons
To help us look for a better way.

The light is always there within
For us to re-ignite,
To penetrate the mist,
Restoring clarity of sight.

Never give up on yourself;
You're the one on whom you should depend.
Regardless of who else is in your life,
You should be your own best friend.

Our struggles can make or break us,
The choice is up to you.
So let them make you stronger…
Know that you can make it through!

Don't ever let anyone bring you down.
Hold your head up high.
Believe that you are capable
Of reaching for the sky.

Remember, you are beautiful
In every single way
And you have every right to be
Proud of who you are today.

WHERE I NEED TO BE

What is the reality?
Was it all just a dream?
I'm no longer definite
That things are as they seem.

Filled with this uncertainty,
I'm sure of nothing that I know
But it's the trials and tribulations
That are meant to help us grow.

So, I'm trusting in you, Universe,
To guide me on my way.
I'm heeding the signs you're sending me
To bring me closer every day.

Accepting, not resisting
Is what will see me free.
I believe that, in this moment,
I'm where I need to be.

THE START OF A NEW WEEK

This isn't a dress rehearsal,
So give all you have to give.
Make the best of every day,
Don't just exist, but live!
Send out love to everyone,
As what you give out comes back to you.
Be there for those who need you
And to yourself, be true.

Every day contains something beautiful,
If you choose to see with your heart;
This is something you should try to remember
As the new week's about to start.
Focus on what's good in life,
Make peace with your past, forgive and forget.
Do what makes you happy
And make this your best week yet!

YIN AND YANG

You can't know real happiness
If you've never been sad.
You can't know true goodness
Until you've experienced something bad.
You can't appreciate ease
If you've never felt pain.
You won't really relish the sunshine
If you've never seen the rain.
You wouldn't see the beauty of night-time
If you've never seen the light of day.
You'd pay no attention to another blue sky
If you'd never seen skies of grey.
You wouldn't understand the power of laughter
If you'd never had reason to cry.
You wouldn't be so grateful for truth and honesty
If you'd never heard a lie.
If you'd never given in to anger
You wouldn't value peace of mind.
You need to be able to recognise
How closely the opposites are entwined.
There'll always be negatives and positives,
Often in equal measure;
But learning to focus on the best points,
Is what gives us a life to treasure.

STEPPING STONES

When things go wrong, what do you do?
Do you carry your mistakes around with you?

Or lay them down as stepping-stones
And make a new path towards the unknown?

When you fall, do you stay down?
Lost at sea, would you just drown?

Or will you allow yourself to soar
And swim for your life, to a new shore?

When, in the wrong direction you stray,
Would you seek to find another way?

Or prefer to simply stay lost,
Afraid of what the search may cost?

Sometimes the right thing's the hardest to do
And you fear it'll bring more pain to you;

But be still and listen to your heart,
The answers you need, it will impart.

Never believe all hope is gone,
There's always a reason to carry on.

LIVE FOR THE DAY

I have no interest in where
The grass may be greener
Or in flying away to where
Skies are more blue.
I am not here to be
In competition with anyone;
No desire to attempt
To be better than you.

All I want is to live
Every day peacefully,
Thankful for all
The blessings in my life;
To be able to find positives
In every adversity;
Free from all
Worries and strife.

Life isn't always
Going to be easy.
Some days we struggle
To go to the lengths
Required to keep moving
Regardless of pain,
Keep our resolve
And find our true strength.

There comes a time
When you finally realise
Life is too short,
You shouldn't waste a day.
So spend time with loved ones;
Be there for each other
And take time to tell them
The things you really want to say.

Because tomorrow is
Promised to no one.
From one day to the next
We know not of our fate.
Be sure people know
How much they mean to you,
Show it today,
Before it's too late.

BEFORE YOUR LIFE IS THROUGH

No one lives forever
So live life while you can.
Time just keeps on passing by;
It waits for no man.

You can waste life thinking 'What if?'
Or wondering what the future will hold.
But while you do, '*now*' is passing you by.
Just allow the future to unfold.

Live life for the moment
And do what you need to do.
Know that you've tried, at least,
Before your life is through.

No point in looking back with regret,
Just simply try your best.
Make all your greatest efforts
Before you're laid to rest.

Step out of your comfort zone.
It may come as a surprise
To discover what you're capable of...
Just how far you can rise.

So embrace opportunities,
Don't let them slip away.
Get the most out of your life
Each and every day.

THE IMPORTANT THINGS IN LIFE

You can be one to make a difference
In a world that's full of strife.
We can't all make massive gestures
But we can be a light in someone's life.

We may never even realise
How much it means to share a smile.
It may be all a person needs
To help them feel that life's worthwhile.

What if you knew that tomorrow
Was to be your very last day?
Would you live it as you've always done
Or spend it in a different way?

Are there people you would contact
To tell them how much they mean to you;
Those you'd want to spend time with
Before your life is through?

Well, the truth is, not any one of us
Can ever really know
So our love for the special people in our lives
Should always be on show.

Don't wait until it's too late
Then have nothing but regret
For not making time for family or friends
Or showing kindness to strangers we met.

You see, true happiness doesn't come
From what we have or how much we earn.
As we keep growing older
There is something that we learn:

That it's people who really matter
And showing love and care.
Not lavish presents and false sentiments
But really being there.

Gifts of friendship, love and laughter
Are things we can all afford to give,
Things you can never run out of
No matter how long you live.

Because the more of these things you give away,
It's absolutely true
They will always be returned
Multiplied, to you.

FULL MOON INTENTIONS

Outside, so peaceful
The only sound, a fox's cry;
Amid a million twinkling diamonds,
A shooting star streaks across the sky.

Enrobed in the darkness
Except for the light of a silvery moon,
I feel my connection to everything
And know that, very soon;

The power of the intentions
That tonight I have set,
Will permeate the Universe
And, I have faith, will be met.

I give thanks for the many blessings
That are in my life every day
And, in advance, for the ones I believe
Are already on their way.

A LESSON FROM NATURE

My garden is such a special place
of beauty – it is my therapy.
Observing it changing, throughout the seasons,
I realise, it is a reflection of me.

Proceeding through Winter – a time of darkness,
where it's easy to believe life has been extinguished,

Moving into Spring – light is returning;
new growth; new beginnings; signs of hope are replenished.

Progress into Summer – the brightest of days,
in which to flourish, develop and continue to grow.

Until we reach Autumn – a time of full maturity,
when at last we can reap what we sow.

No matter how stuck we feel,
we're always moving, transforming.
Our most transitional times come from adversities.

Constantly evolving,
into the next phase.
By hanging on in there, we'll overcome difficulties.

If we persist, we can flourish again.
Keep striving and fighting, refuse to curl up and die.

And always remember:
when the caterpillar thought its life over, it became a butterfly!

LIFE'S MAGIC

There are fairies in my garden!
I know you might not believe
Because I understand for some folk,
It is so hard to perceive.

But when I look out, as the sun fades,
I see sparks of silver light,
Dancing in the darkness
As these little beings take flight.

Running through the blades of grass,
They chase amongst the flowers,
Spreading magic everywhere
With their mystical powers.

A dragon takes them for a ride,
Wings outstretched, whilst breathing fire.
His shadow's seen across the moon
As he keeps soaring higher.

Tiny elves, perched on toadstools,
Sing a merry tune
To a chorus of wolf-bloods
Howling at the moon.

This may have to be our secret.
People would say we're mad!
But when their existence is in doubt,
I think it's rather sad.

When we were young, we'd be happy
To believe such things were true.
That sense of wonder was left behind
Only as we grew.

So why not connect with the child within
And who knows… you just might
Realise, life's still so very full
Of wondrous magic, love and light.

LIFE'S UNFOLDING THE WAY THAT IT SHOULD

Sometimes, in the midst of having life all mapped out,
It seems the Universe has different ideas.
And we feel that life is being unfair,
Resulting in anger and tears.

But, what if instead of resisting the change of direction
We accept it is for our highest good,
As sometimes the Universe works in mysterious ways
That, at first, may not be understood.

The Great Spirit will never close a door on you
Without opening another up wide.
Just keep your eyes focused for where openings appear
And don't be afraid to step inside.

Things may not happen at the exact time that you hope
But they will when the time is right.
It's really important that you don't give in
Before the reward is in sight.

Please don't despair when things don't go your way.
Keep your faith and believe that it's true
That when you think everything's falling apart
There's something better on its way for you.

THE SUN WILL RISE

Tracing a raindrop's trail down the window,
Lit up in the reflection of a candle's flame;
Like the light from your eyes – illuminating
But masking the darkness you'd rather keep hidden.

The howl of the wind blowing through the treetops;
Like a haunting cry for help is riven
Trying desperately to sound strong and forceful
As showing weakness has been forbidden.

Rain falling ever faster and faster,
Like tears escaping from sorrowful eyes.
Unleashed from a cloud that can hold no longer,
Threatens to betray a carefully contrived disguise.

Be patient, eventually the storm is abating;
If we sit tight, the calm will come soon
And a sky once full of angry clouds will clear
Revealing a magical silvery moon.

Storms and darkness never last forever;
Long nights are ended by the sun's rise.
Despair gives way to hope and happiness
As our spirits rise to brighter skies.

FREEDOM

Feeling like a butterfly
That was held within a jar,
She knew exactly how it felt
To be restrained from flying far.

Trapped within this confined space,
Able to see a wider view.
Desperately seeking to spread her wings,
Before her life was through.

She yearned to simply have the chance
To be completely free
And share her beauty with the world –
To be what she was born to be.

Longing for someone to initiate
Her release and let her soar.
She knew that she was capable
Of giving so much more.

One day she would break away
And her spirit would soar so high.
She'd be a source of peace and love
To whomever she passed by.

She'd live life to the fullest
And be the best that she could be;
Doing all the things she dreamed of
And being happy and carefree.

THE STORM

Electrical charges
Illuminate the sky
As Gaia's rage escalates
From way on high.

Unleashing her fury
In a torrent of tears,
Tormented bellows reach crescendo
As the storm nears.

Relentlessly soaking
The Earth to its core
As clouds commence battle
With an almighty roar!

'Til, anger abating,
Her tears subside
And calmness reigns,
So peace may preside.

She paints seven vibrant colours
Overhead in an arc.
Radiating brightness,
Where once was all dark.

THE MAGIC WITHIN

I found a mystical place today
Where fairies, imps and elves did play.
They invited me to dance with them amongst the trees
And witness the magic they did weave.

To locate such a beautiful place
Brought a contented smile to my face.
Marvelling at the majesty of the trees,
Feeling completely happy and carefree.

So next time you're in a forest
And you see a flash of light
Look carefully, for it may just be
A fairy there in flight.

Just because others may doubt,
Don't choose to resist.
Believe with all your heart,
That magic really does exist.

Keep a sense of wonder
And realise it's true
That the real source of magic
Lies inside you!

SIGN OF HOPE

To catch a glimpse of a rainbow
After you've made it through the rain,
Is a sign it's still possible to love your life
Even when you've experienced pain.

It shows you can feel happiness
Even on the hardest day;
A sign that wondrous miracles
Are never far away.

It's a reminder that you are strong
And have the ability to cope
With whatever life sends your way;
So you should never give up hope.

You have a light within you
That can chase darkness away.
At any time, you can change your path
And find a better way.

It's a sign to keep believing
That there's guidance, protection and love.
Your guides are connecting with you
And watching over you from above.

Rainbows are haloes of angels
Letting you know that they're nearby.
See them by not looking down
But keeping your head held high.

GUARDIAN ANGEL

We each have a Guardian Angel
To help guide us on our way,
To protect us and watch over us
As we go about our day.

We need never feel lonely,
Or that we do not have a friend
Because on our Guardian Angel
We can always depend.

Just simply ask for guidance;
Your angel will always hear.
At the times that you really need it
Your angel will always be near.

For whatever you need assistance,
You only have to ask
And your angel is ready and waiting,
Always happy to fulfil the task.

When things seem too much of a struggle
And trouble appears to abound,
Open up your mind to receive the signs
That your angel is around.

A sign will be left to show you,
Maybe a white feather here or there,
Something that you will recognise
And know you have someone who cares.

MINDFULNESS

Sometimes the only companions I need
Are the singing birds, the butterflies and bees.
The sun on my skin, wind tousling my hair;
Easing my mind of worry and care.

The clear blue sky; green grass beneath my feet
In the shelter of the trees, on a wooden park seat.
Apple blossom petals floating gently to the ground,
Feeling like I belong here, true peace of mind is found.

The number of beats our heart contains, no one ever knows
And, no matter how we spend it, the time we have still goes.
So, we may as well spend some of it doing what we love.
Every day is so much better when treated as a gift from above.

So take time out from your busy life
To sit quietly and simply 'be'
And look around with loving eyes
And be amazed by the beauty you see.

SURVIVE AND THRIVE TOGETHER

Sedum said, 'I was the flower they chose.
I was planted here.'
To the poppy, growing wild,
'You don't belong!' he'd sneer.

Poppy stood, bud tightly shut,
Afraid to give reply;
Until a bee overheard
As he bumbled by.

'Pay no heed to unkindness,'
He whispered to the flower.
'Stand firm and strong, raise your head;
Don't give anyone your power!'

Silently, she listened
To the kind bee's every word
And gradually she realised,
To give in would be absurd.

And so, with each new day that dawned,
She gained strength, more and more.
Until, to stay tight as a bud,
Was wrong, she felt, for sure.

It was her time to bloom now
So, her petals she unfurled.
Afraid no longer to reveal
Her inner beauty to the world.

Sedum gasped and he remarked,
'You're a beauty to behold
And I was only being unkind,
If the truth be told...

'Because we appear so different,
I thought we couldn't get along
But I hope that you'll forgive me
As I accept that I was wrong!'

Poppy said, 'You are forgiven;
We're not so different, you and I.
Despite outward appearances,
We can live in harmony.'

They continue to grow together
To flourish and to thrive
And we must learn to do the same
If humanity is to survive.

BLESSINGS

Taking a few moments to sit in silence
At the end of the day,
Here in my garden, where
In the dusk the fairies play.

I watch in awe and wonder
At this magical sight –
Their tiny, sparkling gossamer wings,
Twinkling in the moonlight.

The world is full of wonders
That we don't always see
Because we're too busy 'doing'
Instead of taking time to simply 'be'.

So, if you really want to notice
All the miracles that abound,
Stop, listen and look with your heart
And you'll find them all around.

Don't forget to give thanks for the blessings
That have already been sent your way,
And pray that you will wake again
To face another beautiful day.

Then sleep soundly, knowing your angels
Are watching over you from above
And that you are safe and protected
Surrounded by their unconditional love.

OUR HIGHER SELF

Sometimes the tears have to fall, to wash away the pain,
To cleanse the soul.
Sometimes we need to be still and listen for the answers,
To help us become whole.

Our deepest despair is often what
Empowers us to grow
Into our higher selves; to follow
The Universal Flow.

Don't always question what's being sent your way,
It will be for the highest good.
Sometimes we just have to accept. Not everything
Needs to be understood.

It will become clear in the fullness of time,
Whatever happens, there's always a reason.
Some things are meant for a life-time,
Some only for a season.

Trust your own instincts, believe that the truth
Always lies within your heart.
And never fear when darkness descends,
Each day brings a brand new start.

ONE MORE SUNRISE

Watching poppy heads swaying in the gentle breeze
Sitting under a diamond-studded sky,
I'm sure I see fairies dancing amongst the trees
And hear an angel's sigh.
Snails leaving trails of silver thread
That sparkle in the moonlight.
Night creatures stealthily tread,
It's such a magical night!

It's so beautiful outside on nights like these;
Lilac scent hanging in the air.
Right now I've found perfect peace;
There's not a sound anywhere.
Time for reflection at the end of the day
In which we've made more happy memories.
Dear Universe, thanks for the blessings you sent my way,
Grant me another sunrise to view, please...

SOLITUDE AND SILENCE

Listening to the rain pattering;
Wind swirling through the trees.
Sitting in solitude and silence
The Earth's music my mind does ease.

The sound of one's own heart and breath
Following their own rhythmic beat.
Allowing solitude and silence,
My own demons I'll defeat.

What does it say about a person
Who's not happy in their own company?
I permit solitude and silence
To encompass me.

What else is there for me to hear?
A serenade from the birds…
Nature's chorus speaks more to me
Than a million words.

Solitude and silence;
True wisdom, they impart.
In those moments I can find
Such peace inside my heart.

Never be too busy following,
Always use your own free will.
Enjoy solitude and silence
And make time to just be still.

GRATITUDE AT THE END OF THE DAY

There's no better way of finishing
A day that is done,
Than sitting, relaxing, peacefully
Watching the setting sun.

Swifts gliding and swooping;
Circling overhead.
Calling to each other,
'Stop playing, it's time for bed.'

The heady scent of honeysuckle
And lavender in the air;
Nature's calming perfumes,
To which nothing can compare.

As dusk falls upon us,
Bats flutter by
And a million tiny diamonds
Light up the darkened sky.

A silver light is cast,
By the rising moon.
As eyes grow wearier, we know
Sleep is coming soon.

So many beautiful moments
From the day we've left behind.
So much to be thankful for –
Memories to treasure in our mind.

Heading into sweet dreams
As we gently drift away,
Into peaceful slumber
Leading to a bright new day.

A BETTER WORLD

I was soaring over the sea last night,
As free as a bird that's taken flight.
White horses prancing beneath my feet
As I rose through the clouds to a heavenly retreat.

Breaking away from the Earth below,
Enveloped in an angelic glow;
Floating on air, so feather light,
To a brand new world, peaceful and bright.

A place beyond worry, fear and pain,
Where no one would ever suffer again.
No killing or fighting in needless wars,
Everyone working only for the greatest cause.

Accepting each other, letting each other be.
Every person, happy and free
To have their own beliefs, yet still tolerate
Those who see differently – there's no room for hate.

Then I was told I must return to Earth,
It was the time of my re-birth.
But I must take with me the peace of above.
My mission was to spread harmony and love.

Sadly, as I did awake,
I felt as if my heart would break
To find things were not as they seem
And it was, in fact, all just a dream.

So I vowed from that moment on
I would view everybody as if we are One.
With respect, everyone I would treat
And show kindness to all that I meet.

Once we all realise peace comes from within
That's when Earth's healing will really begin.
Look at our own actions, we need to comprehend
That this is how the ripple will extend.

Ensure it is only good seeds that you sow
And the wave of peace, love and harmony will grow.
You can play your part and do all that you can
To make a better world for you and your fellow man.

www.ingramcontent.com/pod-product-compliance
Lightning Source LLC
Chambersburg PA
CBHW020037040426
42331CB00031B/946